LENGAGE Learning

# Drama for Students, Volume 2

## STAFF

David Galens and Lynn M. Spampinato, *Editors*

Thomas Allbaugh, Craig Bentley, Terry Browne, Christopher Busiel, Stephen Coy, L. M. Domina, John Fiero, Carol L. Hamilton, Erika Kreger, Jennifer Lewin, Sheri Metzger, Daniel Moran, Terry Nienhuis, Bonnie Russell, Arnold Schmidt, William Wiles, Joanne Woolway, *Contributing Writers*

Elizabeth Cranston, Kathleen J. Edgar, Joshua Kondek, Marie Lazzari, Tom Ligotti, Marie Napierkowski, Scot Peacock, Mary Ruby, Diane Telgen, Patti Tippett, Kathleen Wilson, Pam Zuber, *Contributing Editors*

Pamela Wilwerth Aue, *Managing Editor*

Jeffery Chapman, *Programmer/Analyst*

Victoria B. Cariappa, *Research Team Manager*
Michele P. LaMeau, Andy Guy Malonis, Barb

McNeil, Gary Oudersluys, Maureen Richards, *Research Specialists*

Julia C. Daniel, Tamara C. Nott, Tracie A. Richardson, Cheryl L. Warnock, *Research Associates*

Susan M. Trosky, *Permissions Manager*
Kimberly F. Smilay, *Permissions Specialist*
Sarah Chesney, *Permissions Associate*
Steve Cusack, Kelly A. Quin, *Permissions Assistants*

Mary Beth Trimper, *Production Director*
Evi Seoud, *Assistant Production Manager*
Shanna Heilveil, *Production Assistant*

Randy Bassett, *Image Database Supervisor*
Mikal Ansari, Robert Duncan, *Imaging Specialists*
Pamela A. Reed, *Photography Coordinator*

Cynthia Baldwin, *Product Design Manager*
Cover design: Michelle DiMercurio, *Art Director*
Page design: Pamela A. E. Galbreath, *Senior Art Director*

Since this page cannot legibly accommodate all copyright notices, the acknowledgments constitute an extension of the copyright notice.

While every effort has been made to secure permission to reprint material and to ensure the reliability of the information presented in this publication, Gale Research neither guarantees the accuracy of the data contained herein nor assumes any responsibility for errors, omissions, or discrepancies. Gale accepts no payment for listing;

and inclusion in the publication of any organization, agency, institution, publication, service, or individual does not imply endorsement of the editors or publisher. Errors brought to the attention of the publisher and verified to the satisfaction of the publisher will be corrected in future editions.

This publication is a creative work fully protected by all applicable copyright laws, as well as by misappropriation, trade secret, unfair competition, and other applicable laws. The authors and editors of this work have added value to the underlying factual material herein through one or more of the following: unique and original selection, coordination, expression, arrangement, and classification of the information.

All rights to this publication will be vigorously defended.

Copyright © 1998
Gale Research
835 Penobscot Building
645 Griswold St.
Detroit, MI 48226-4094

All rights reserved including the right of reproduction in whole or in part in any form.

This book is printed on acid-free paper that meets the minimum requirements of American National Standard for Information Sciences—Permanence Paper for Printed Library Materials, ANSI Z39.48-1984.

ISBN 0-7876-1684-2

ISSN applied for and pending
Printed in the United States of America
10 9 8 7 6 5 4 3

# *Crimes of the Heart*

Beth Henley

1979

## Introduction

Beth Henley completed *Crimes of the Heart,* her tragic comedy about three sisters surviving crisis after crisis in a small Mississippi town, in 1978. She submitted it to several regional theatres for consideration without success. Unknown to her, however, a friend had entered it in the well-known Great American Play Contest of the Actors' Theatre of Louisville. The play was chosen as co-winner for 1977-78 and performed in February, 1979, at the company's annual festival of New American Plays. The production was extremely well-received, and the play was picked up by numerous regional theatres for their 1979-81 seasons.

At the end of 1980, *Crimes of the Heart* was produced off-Broadway at the Manhattan Theatre Club for a limited, sold-out, engagement of thirty-two performances. By the time the play transferred to Broadway in November, 1981, *Crimes of the Heart* had received the prestigious Pulitzer Prize. Henley was the first woman to win the Pulitzer for Drama in twenty-three years, and her play was the first ever to win before opening on Broadway. *Crimes of the Heart* went on to garner the New York Drama Critics Circle Award for Best New American Play, a Gugenheim Award, and a Tony nomination. The tremendously successful Broadway production ran for 535 performances, spawning regional productions in London, Chicago, Washington, Atlanta, Los Angeles, Dallas, and Houston. The success of the play—and especially the prestige of the Pulitzer award—assured Henley's place among the elite of the American theatre for years to come. As Henley herself put it, with typically wry humor, "winning the Pulitzer Prize means I'll never have to work in a dog-food factory again" (Haller 44).

Often compared to the work of other "Southern Gothic" writers like Eudora Welty and Flannery O'Connor, Henley's play is widely appreciated for its compassionate look at good country people whose lives have gone wrong. Henley explores the pain of life by piling up tragedies on her characters in a manner some critics have found excessive, but she does so with a dark and penetrating sense of humor which audiences—as the play's success has demonstrated—found to be a fresh perspective in the American theatre.

# Author Biography

Beth Henley was born May 8, 1952, in Jackson, Mississippi, the daughter of an attorney and a community theatre actress. Her southern heritage has played a large role in the setting and themes of her writing, as well as the critical response she has received—she is often categorized as a writer of the "Southern Gothic" tradition. As an undergraduate at Southern Methodist University (SMU) in Dallas, Texas, Henley studied acting and this training has remained important to her since her transition to play writing. Directors and fellow playwrights have observed that Henley "approaches a play from the point of view of theater, not literature" and that "as an actress, she then knows how to make her works stageworthy" (Haller).

She wrote her first play, a one-act titled *Am I Blue,* to fulfill a play writing class assignment. When it was produced at SMU her senior year, she modestly used the pseudonym Amy Peach. The play has an adolescent perspective—two insecure and lonely teenagers meet in a squalid section of New Orleans—but audiences and critics (who reviewed the play when it was revived in 1981) found in it many of the themes, and much of the promise, of Henley's later work. Henley undertook graduate study at the University of Illinois, where she taught acting and voice technique. By this time, however, she was growing more interested in writing, primarily out of a frustration at the lack of good contemporary roles for southern women.

Henley completed *Crimes of the Heart* in 1978 and submitted it for production consideration, without success, to several regional theatres. The play was eventually produced in the Actors' Theatre of Louisville's 1979 Festival of New Plays. The successful production in this prestigious festival led to several regional productions, an off-Broadway production at the Manhattan Theatre Club, and a Pulitzer Prize for Drama, unprecedented for a play which had not yet opened on Broadway. When it did, in November, 1981, the play was a smash success, playing for 535 performances and spawning many other successful regional productions. When *Crimes of the Heart* was made into a film in 1986 it received mixed reviews, but Henley did receive an Academy Award nomination for her screenplay adaptation.

With the prestige of the Pulitzer Prize and all the acclaim afforded *Crimes of the Heart*—her first full-length play—Henley was catapulted to success in the contemporary American theatre. The attention paid to her also, however, put extreme pressure on her to succeed at that level. As Henley said of the Pulitzer: "Later on they make you pay for it" (Betsko and Koenig 215). Many critics have been hard on Henley's later plays, finding none of them equal to the creativity of *Crimes of the Heart*. Her second full-length play, *The Miss Firecracker Contest* was, however, predominantly well-received. Similarly a dark comedy about a small Mississippi town, the play was completed in 1980, and premiered in several regional productions in 1981-82 before opening at the Manhattan Theatre Club in 1984. It played off-Broadway for a total of 244 performances, moving to larger quarters in the process. *The Miss Firecracker Contest* was adapted into a film in 1988, starring Holly Hunter.

In October, 1982, *The Wake of Jamey Foster,* Henley's third full-length play, closed on Broadway after only twelve performances. Henley felt that this commercial flop (not uncommon under the severe financial pressures of Broadway production) was "part of the cost of winning" the Pulitzer Prize (Betsko and Koenig 215). Her next play, *The Debutante Ball,* was better received, and throughout the last decade Henley has remained a productive and successful writer for Broadway, the regional theatres, and film. Her major projects include the plays *The Lucky Spot, Abundance,* and *Control Freaks.* She also wrote the screenplay for *Nobody's Fool* (as well as screen adaptations of her own plays) and collaborated with Budge Threlkeld on the Public Broadcasting System's *Survival Guides* and with David Byrne and Stephen Tobolowsky on the screenplay for Byrne's 1986 film *True Stories.*

# Plot Summary

The entire action of the play takes place in the kitchen of the MaGrath sisters' house in Hazlehurst, Mississippi

## *Act I*

The action opens on Lenny McGrath trying to stick a birthday candle into a cookie. Her cousin, Chick, arrives, upset about news in the paper (the content of which is not yet revealed to the audience). She wonders how she's "gonna continue holding my head up high in this community." She and Lenny discuss going to pick up Lenny's sister Babe. Chick expresses displeasure with other facets of the MaGraths' family, as she gives Lenny a birthday present—a box of candy. Doc Porter, an old boyfriend of the other McGrath sister, Meg, arrives, and Chick leaves to pick up Babe. Lenny is upset at Doc's news that Billy Boy, an old childhood horse of Lenny's, was struck by lightning and killed. Doc leaves to pick up his son at the dentist.

Lenny receives a phone call with news about "Zackery" (who we learn later is Babe's husband), who is hospitalized with serious injuries. Meg arrives, and as she and Lenny talk, it is revealed that Babe has shot her husband and is being held in jail. There is an awkwardness between the two sisters as they discuss their grandfather; Lenny has been caring for him (sleeping on a cot in the kitchen to be near his room), and he has recently been hospitalized after a stroke. Lenny learns that Meg's singing career, the reason she had moved to California, is not going well—as is evidenced by her return to Hazelhurst.

Chick returns to the house, accompanying Babe. Chick shows obvious displeasure for Meg, and for Babe, who "doesn't understand how serious the situation is." Lenny and Chick run out after a phone call from a neighbor having an emergency. Meg and Babe, left alone together, discuss why it was that their mother committed suicide, hanging herself along with the family cat. Babe also begins revealing to her sister more about shooting her husband. The sisters also discuss Lenny, whose self-consciousness over her shrunken ovary, they feel, has prevented her from pursuing relationships with men, in particular a Charlie from Memphis who Lenny dated briefly. Noticing the box of candy, Meg and Babe realize they've forgotten Lenny's birthday. They plan to order her a cake, as Babe's lawyer Barnette arrives at the house. Babe hides from him at first, as Meg and Barnette, who remembers her singing days in Biloxi, become reacquainted.

Barnette reveals that he's taken Babe's case partly because he has a personal vendetta against Zackery, Babe's husband. Barnette also reveals that medical records suggest Zackery had abused Meg leading up to the shooting. Barnette leaves and Babe reappears, confronted by Meg with the medical information. Babe admits she's protecting someone: Willie Jay, a fifteen year-old African American boy with whom Babe had been having an affair. The shooting, Babe says, was a result of her anger after Zackery threatened Willie Jay and pushed him down the porch steps. As the act ends, Babe agrees to cooperate with Barnette for the benefit of her case, and the two sisters plan a belated birthday celebration for Lenny.

## *Act II*

Evening of the same day. Barnette is interviewing Babe about the case. Babe says after the shooting her mouth was "just as dry as a bone" so she went to the kitchen and made a pitcher of lemonade. She is afraid that this detail is "gonna look kinda bad." Zackery calls, threatening that he has evidence damaging to Babe. Barnette leaves to meet him at the hospital, after answering Babe's question about the nature of his personal vendetta against Zack: "the major thing he did was to ruin my father's life."

Lenny enters, fuming; Meg, apparently, lied "shamelessly" to their grandfather about her career in show business. Old jealousies resurface; Lenny asks Babe about Meg: "why should Old Grandmama let her sew twelve golden jingle bells on her petticoats and us only three?" Babe and Lenny discuss the hurricane which wiped out Biloxi, when Doc's leg was severely injured after his roof caved in. Many people have the perception, apparently, that Meg, refusing to evacuate,"baited Doc into staying there with her."

Meg enters, with a bottle of bourbon from which she has already been drinking. An apology for her lying to grandpa is quickly forthcoming, but she says "I just wasn't going to sit there and look at him all miserable and sick and sad!" The three sisters look through an old photo album. Enjoying one another's company at last, they decide to play cards, when Doc phones and is invited over by Meg. Lenny begins criticizing Meg, who counters by asking Lenny about Charlie; Lenny gets angry at Babe for having revealed this secret to Meg. Meg continues to push the point, and Lenny runs upstairs, sobbing. Babe follows, to comfort her.

At this less than opportune moment, Doc arrives. He and Meg drink together, and talk about the hurricane and hard times. Meg reveals to Doc that she "went insane" in L.A. and ended up in the psychiatric ward of the country hospital. The two decide to go off together and continue to drink; there is an obvious attraction, but Doc is careful to say they're "just gonna look at the moon" and not get in over their heads. There is a knock at the back door, and Babe comes downstairs to admit Barnette. He has bad news for Babe: Zackery's sister, suspicious of Babe, had hired a detective, who produced compromising photographs of Babe with Willie Jay. Babe is devastated, and as a final blow to close the act, Lenny comes downstairs to report that the hospital has called with news that their grandfather has suffered another stroke.

# Act III

The following morning. Babe enters and lies down on Lenny's cot. Lenny enters, also weary. Chick's voice is heard almost immediately; her questions reveal that grandpa is in a coma and will likely not live. Chick and Lenny divide between them a list of people they must "notify about Old Granddaddy's predicament." Chick goes off with obvious displeasure with the sisters. Lenny and Babe ruminate about when Meg might be coming home.

Meg actually returns a moment later, exuberant. Exhausted by their traumatic night, Lenny and Babe break down in hysterical laughter telling Meg the news about their grandfather. As the three sisters talk, Meg and Babe convince Lenny to call her man Charlie and restart their relationship. With her confidence up, Lenny goes upstairs to make the call. Babe shows Meg the envelope of incriminating photographs.

Barnette arrives; he states that he's been able to dig up enough scandal about Zackery to force him to settle the case out of court. In order to keep the photos of Babe and Willie Jay secret, however, he will not be able to expose Zackery openly, which had been his original hope and intention. Willie Jay, meanwhile, will be sent North to live in safety. Barnette leaves; so does Meg, to pick up Lenny's late birthday cake.

Lenny comes downstairs, frustrated at having been too self-conscious to call Charlie. Chick arrives a moment later, calling Meg a "low-class tramp" for going off with Doc. Lenny confronts Chick and tells her to leave; she does, but continues to curses the family as Lenny chases her out the door. Zackery calls, informing Babe he's going to have her committed to a mental institution. She defies him to do so and hangs up the phone, but she is clearly disturbed by the threat. Lenny re-enters, elated at her triumph over Chick, and decides to make another try at calling Charlie. Babe takes rope from a drawer and goes upstairs.

Lenny makes the call; it goes well, and she makes a date with him for that evening. Wanting to tell someone, she runs out back to find Babe. There is a thud from upstairs; Babe comes down with a broken piece of rope around her neck. She makes another attempt to commit suicide, on-stage, by sticking her head in the oven. Meg finds her there and pulls her out. Babe, feeling enlightened, says she knows why their mother killed the cat along with herself; not because she hated it but because she loved it and "was afraid of dying all alone." Meg comforts Babe by convincing her Zackery won't be able to make good on his threat. Lenny returns and is surprised by her sisters with a late birthday celebration. Despite the many troubles hanging over them, the play ends with the MaGrath sisters smiling and laughing together for a moment, in "a magical, golden, sparkling glimmer."

# Characters

## Babe

Babe is the youngest MaGrath sister. At the start of the play, she has shot her husband, Zackery, a powerful and wealthy lawyer. At first, the only explanation she gives for the act is the defiant statement: "I didn't like his looks! I just didn't like his stinking looks!" Eventually, she reveals that the shooting was the result of her anger at Zackery's cruel treatment both of her and of Willie Jay, a fifteen year-old African American boy with whom Babe had been carrying on an affair.

Babe makes two attempts to kill herself late in the play. After being rescued by Meg, Babe appears enlightened and at peace with her mother's suicide. Babe says she understands why their mother hanged the family cat along with herself; not because she hated it but because she loved it and "was afraid of dying all alone."

## Becky

*See* Babe

## Rebecca Botrelle

*See* Babe

## Chick Boyle

The sisters' first cousin, who is twenty-nine years old. She is a very demanding relative, extremely concerned about the community's opinion of her. When news is published of Babe's shooting of Zackery, Chick's primary concern is how she's "gonna continue holding my head up high in this community." Chick is critical of all aspects of the MaGrath's family and is always bringing up past tragedies such as the mother's suicide. Chick is especially hard on Meg, whom she finds undisciplined and calls a "low-class tramp," and on Babe, who "doesn't understand how serious the situation is" after shooting Zackery. Chick seems to feel closest to Lenny, and is genuinely surprised to be ushered out of the house for her comments about Lenny's sisters.

## Barnette Lloyd

Barnette is Babe's lawyer. An ambitious, talented attorney, Barnette views Babe's case as a chance to exact his personal revenge on Zackery. "The major thing he did," Barnette says, "was to ruin my father's life." Barnette also seems to have a strong attraction to Babe, whom he remembers distinctly from a chance meeting at a Christmas bazaar. Barnette is prevented from taking on Zackery in open court by the desire to protect Babe's affair with Willie Jay from public exposure. He is willing to make this sacrifice for Babe, and the play ends with some hope that his efforts will be rewarded.

## Lenny MaGrath

Lenny, at the age of thirty, is the oldest MaGrath sister. Her sisters have forgotten her birthday, only compounding her sense of rejection. Lenny is frustrated after years of carrying heavy burdens of responsibility; most recently, she has been caring for Old Granddaddy, sleeping on a cot in the kitchen to be near him. Lenny loves her sisters but is also jealous of them, especially Meg, whom she feels received preferential treatment during their upbringing. Meg has also been surrounded by men all her life, while Lenny has feared rejection from the opposite sex and become withdrawn as a result. She fears continuing the one romantic relationship, with a Charlie Hill from Memphis, which has gone well for her in recent years.

While almost continuously pushed beyond the point of frustration, Lenny nevertheless has a close bond of loyalty with her sisters. Chick is constantly criticizing the family (culminating in her calling Meg a "low-class tramp"); when Lenny is finally pushed to the point that she turns on her cousin, chasing her out of the house with a broom, this is an important turning point in the play. It demonstrates the ultimate strength of family bonds—and their social value—in Henley's play.

## Meg MaGrath

Meg is the middle sister at twenty-seven years of age. As an eleven year-old child, Meg discovered the body of their mother (and that of the family cat) following her suicide. This traumatic experience provoked Meg to test her strength by confronting morbidity wherever she could find it, including poring over medical photographs of disease-ridden victims and staring at March of Dimes posters of crippled children. At the beginning of the play Meg returns to Mississippi from Los Angeles, where her singing career has stalled and where, she later tells Doc, she had a nervous breakdown and ended up in the psychiatric ward of the county hospital.

## Media Adaptations

- *Crimes of the Heart* was adapted as a film in 1986, directed by Bruce Beresford and starring Diane Keaton, Jessica Lange, Sissy Spacek, and Sam Shepard. The film adds as fully-realized characters several people who are only discussed in the play: Old Granddaddy, Zackery and Willie Jay. The film received decidedly mixed reviews but also garnered three Academy Award nominations, for Henley's screenplay and for the acting of Spacek and Tess Harper, who played the catty Chick.

- In a rare example of reverse adaptation from drama to fiction, Claudia Reilly published in 1986 a novel, *Crimes of the Heart,* based on Henley's play.

---

The other MaGrath sisters share a perception that Meg has always received preferential treatment in life. When Lenny ponders "why should Old Grandmama let her sew twelve golden jingle bells on her petticoats and us only three?" this is not a minor issue for her and Babe. The two sisters feel on some level that this special treatment has led Meg to act irresponsibly—as when she abandoned Doc, for whatever reason, after he was severely injured in the hurricane. Lenny is angry with Meg for lying to Old Granddaddy in the hospital about her career, but Meg states "I just wasn't going to sit there and look at him all miserable and sick and sad!" Both Babe and Lenny are concerned when Meg disappears with Doc her first night back in Mississippi. Both sisters, however—especially

Lenny—are also protective of Meg, especially from the attacks of their cousin Chick.

## *Rebecca MaGrath*

*See* Babe

## *Doc Porter*

Doc is Meg's old boyfriend. He is still known affectionately as "Doc" although his plans for a medical career stalled and eventually died after he was severely injured in Hurricane Camille—his love for Meg (and her promise to marry him) prompted him to stay behind with her while the rest of the town evacuated the storm's path. Many people now have the perception (as Meg and Lenny discuss) that Meg "baited Doc into staying there with her." Doc, who now has his own wife and children, nevertheless remains close to the MaGrath family. Although Meg abandoned him when she left for California, Doc remains fond of her, and Meg is extremely happy to have his friendship upon her return from California.

# Themes

## *Absurdity*

Much like the playwrights of the Theatre of the Absurd, Henley dramatizes a vision of a disordered universe in which characters are isolated from one another and are incapable of meaningful action. With the constant frustration of their dreams and hopes, Henley's characters could easily find their lives completely meaningless and absurd (and indeed, each of the MaGrath sisters has been on the brink of giving up entirely). At the end of *Crimes of the Heart,* at least, the sisters have found a kind of unity in the face of adversity. While Lenny's vision, "something about the three of us smiling and laughing together," in no way can resolve the many conflicts that have unfolded in the course of the play, it does endow their lives with a collective sense of hope, where before each had felt acutely the absurdity, and often the hopelessness, of life.

# Topics for Further Study

- Research the destructive effects of Hurricane "Camille," which in 1969 traveled 1,800 kilometers along a broad arc from Louisiana to Virginia. Why do you think Henley chose to set *Crimes of the Heart* in the shadow, as it were, of this Hurricane? What does Camille represent for each of the major characters and thematically to the play as a whole?

- Consider Babe's legal position at the end of the play. What do you think is likely to happen to her? Draw from your understanding of Barnette's case against Zackery and Zackery's case against Babe. From your own perspective, how do you think Babe will change as a result of this event and what do you feel her future should rightly be?

- Contrast Lenny's and Meg's life strategies: how do they each view responsibility, career, family, romance? How spontaneous—or not —is each one? What are the strongest bonds between the sisters, and what are their sources of conflict?

- Research the prestige of the Pulitzer Prizes and the history of the Pulitzer for Drama—you might begin with Thomas P. Adler's book *Mirror on the Stage: The Pulitzer Plays as an Approach to American Drama.* When Henley won the Pulitzer for Drama in 1981, who was the last woman who had won the prize, twenty-three years earlier? Why did winning the Pulitzer draw so much attention to Henley, as it did to Marsha Norman two years later, when she won with her play *'Night, Mother?*

## *Death*

Reminders of death are everywhere in *Crimes of the Heart:* the sisters are haunted by the memory of their mother's suicide; Babe has shot and seriously wounded her husband; Lenny learns that her beloved childhood horse has been struck by lightning and killed; Old Granddaddy has a second stroke and is apparently near death; Babe attempts suicide twice near the end of the play. Perhaps even stronger than these reminders of physical death, however, are the images of emotional or spiritual death in the play. Lenny, for example, has rejected Charlie, her only suitor in recent years, because she feels worthless and fears rejection herself. Meg, meanwhile, has experienced a psychotic episode in Los Angeles and has prevented herself from loving anyone in order to avoid feeling vulnerable. Significant transitions occur near the end of the play, individual "rebirths" which preface the significant rebirth of a sense of unity among the sisters: Lenny gains the courage to call her suitor, and finds him receptive; Meg, in the course of spending a night out with Doc, is surprised to learn that she "could care about someone," and sings "all night long" out of joy; and finally, Babe has a moment of enlightenment in which she understands that their mother hanged the family cat along with herself because "she was afraid of dying all alone." This revelation allows her to put to rest finally the painful memory of the mother's suicide, and paves the way for the moment of sisterly love at the conclusion of the play.

## *Good and Evil*

Henley challenges the audience's sense of

good and evil by making them like characters who have committed crimes of passion. "I thought I'd like to write about somebody who shoots somebody else just for being mean," Henley said in *Saturday Review*. "Then I got intrigued with the idea of the audience's not finding fault with her character, finding sympathy for her." While Babe's case constitutes the primary exploration of good and evil in the play, the conflict between Meg and her sisters is another example of Henley presenting a number of perspectives on a character's actions in order to complicate her audience's notions of good and bad behavior. Lenny and Babe find many of Meg's actions (abandoning Doc after his accident, lying to Granddaddy about her career in Hollywood) to be dishonest and selfish, but the sisters eventually learn to understand Meg's motivations and to forgive her. Through this process, Henley suggests the sheer complexity of human psychology and behavior— that often, actions cannot be easily labeled "good" or "evil" in a strict sense.

## *Limitations and Opportunities*

Virtually all the characters, to some extent, have throughout their lives been limited in their choices, experiencing a severe lack of opportunity. Lenny, in particular, resents having had to take upon herself so much responsibility for the family (especially for Old Granddaddy). Much of Babe's difficulty in her marriage to Zackery, meanwhile, seems to have grown out the fact that she did not choose him but was pressured by her grandfather into marrying the successful lawyer. Meg, however, at least to Lenny and Babe, appears to have had endless opportunity. Lenny wonders at one point: "Why, do you remember how Meg always got to wear twelve jingle bells on her petticoats, while we were only allowed to wear three apiece? Why?!" Lenny is clearly fixating on a minor issue from childhood, but one she feels is representative of the preferential treatment Meg received. The bells are, she says to Meg later, a "specific example of how you always got what you wanted!" Meg, however, has learned a hard lesson in Hollywood about opportunity and success. Old Granddaddy has always told her: "With your talent, all you need is exposure. Then you can make your own breaks!" Contrary to this somewhat simplistic optimism, however, Meg's difficulty sustaining a singing career suggests that opportunity is actually quite rare, and not necessarily directly connected to talent or one's will to succeed.

## *Public vs. Private Life*

When Babe reveals to Meg her affair with Willie Jay, she admits that she's "so worried about his getting public exposure." This is a necessary concern for public opinion, as Willie Jay might physically be in danger as a result of such exposure. Chick, meanwhile, has what Henley characterizes as an unhealthy concern for public perception—she cares much more about what the rest of the town thinks of her than she does about any of her cousins. Immediately upon her entrance at the beginning of the play, Chick focuses not so much upon Babe's shooting of Zackery, but rather on how the event will affect her, personally:"How I'm gonna continue holding my head up high in this community, I do not know." Similarly, in criticizing Meg for abandoning Doc, Chick thinks primarily of her own public stature: "Well, his mother was going to keep *me* out of the Ladies' Social League because of it." Near the end of the play, Lenny becomes infuriated over Chick calling Meg "a low-class tramp," and chases her cousin out of the house. This moment of family solidarity is a significant turning point, in which Lenny clearly indicates that the private, family unity the three sisters are able to achieve by the end of the play is far more important than the public perception of the family within the town.

## *Violence and Cruelty*

Accompanying the exploration of good and evil in *Crimes of the Heart* are its insights into violence and cruelty. While Babe has ostensibly committed the most violent act in the play by shooting Zackery in the stomach, the audience is persuaded to side with her in the face of the violence wrought by Zackery upon both Babe (domestic violence stemming, as Babe says, from him "hating me, 'cause I couldn't laugh at his jokes"), and, in a jealous rage, on Willie Jay. There occur other, less prominent acts of cruelty in the course of the play, as well as numerous ones the audience learns about through exposition (such as Meg's abandonment of Doc following his injury).

In the end, Henley encourages the audience to take a less absolute view of what constitutes cruelty, to understand some of the underlying reasons behind the actions of her characters, and to join in the sense of forgiveness and acceptance which dominates the conclusion of *Crimes of the Heart*.

# Style

Set in the small southern town of Hazlehurst, Mississippi, *Crimes of the Heart* centers on three sisters who converge at the house of their grandfather after the youngest, Babe, has shot her husband following years of abuse. The other sisters have their own difficulties—Meg's Hollywood singing career is a bust, and Lenny (the eldest) is frustrated and lonely after years of bearing familial responsibility (most recently, she has been sleeping on a cot in the kitchen in order to care for the sisters' ailing grandfather). Over the course of two days, the sisters endure a number of conflicts, both between themselves and with other characters. In the end, however, they manage to come together in a moment of unity and joy despite their difficulties.

Beth Henley is most often praised, especially regarding *Crimes of the Heart,* for the creative blending of different theatrical styles and moods which gives her plays a unique perspective on small-town life in the South. Her multi-faceted approach to dramatic writing is underscored by the rather eclectic group of playwrights Henley once listed for an interviewer as being her major influences: Anton Chekhov, William Shakespeare, Eugene O'Neill, Tennessee Williams, Samuel Beckett, David Mamet, Henrik Ibsen, Lillian Hellman, and Carson McCullers. In particular, Henley's treatment of the tragic and grotesque with humor startled audiences and critics (who were either pleasantly surprised, or unpleasantly shocked). While this macabre humor is often associated with the Southern Gothic movement in literature, Henley's dramatic technique is difficult to qualify as being strongly of one theatrical bent or another. For example, *Crimes of the Heart* has many of the characteristics of a naturalistic work of the "well-made play" tradition: a small cast, a single set, a three-act structure, an initial conflict which is complicated in the second act and resolved in the third. As Scott Haller observed in *Saturday Review,* however, Henley's purpose is not the resurrection of this tradition but the "ransacking" of it. "In effect," he wrote, "she has mated the conventions of the naturalistic play with the unconventional protagonists of absurdist comedy. It is this unlikely dramatic alliance, plus her vivid Southern vernacular, that supplies Henley's idiosyncratic voice."

The rapid accumulation of tragedies in Henley's dramatic world thus appears too absurd to be real, yet too tangibly real to be absurd, and therein lies the playwright's originality. Many critics have joined Haller in finding in Henley's work elements of the Theatre of the Absurd, which presented a vision of a disordered universe in which characters are isolated from one another and are incapable of meaningful action. There is, however, much more specificity to the plot and lives of the characters in *Crimes of the Heart* than there is, for example, in a play by absurdists like Beckett or Eugene Ionesco. Nevertheless, Henley shares with these playwrights, and others of the Absurd, a need to express the dark humor inherent in the struggle to create meaning out of life.

Henley's macabre sense of humor has resulted in frequent comparisons to Southern Gothic writers such as Flannery O'Connor and Eudora Welty. Providing a theatrical rationale for much of what appears to be impossibly eccentric behavior on the part of Henley's characters; in the *New York Times,* Walter Kerr wrote: "We do understand the ground-rules of matter-of-fact Southern grotesquerie, and we know that they're by no means altogether artificial. People do such things and, having done them, react in surprising ways." Although Henley once stated that when she began writing plays she was not familiar with O'Connor, and that she "didn't consciously" say that she "was going to be like Southern Gothic or grotesque," she has since read widely among the work of O'Connor and others, and agrees the connections are there. Of her eccentric brand of humor Henley, quoted in *Mississippi Writers Talking,* suspected that "I guess maybe that's just inbred in the South. You hear people tell stories, and somehow they are always more vivid and violent than the stories people tell out in Los Angeles."

While *Crimes of the Heart* does have a tightly-structured plot, with a central and several tangential conflicts, Henley's real emphasis, as Nancy Hargrove suggested in the *Southern Quarterly,* is "on character rather than on action." Jon Jory, the director of the original Louisville production, observes that what so impressed him initially about

Henley's play was her "immensely sensitive and complex view of relationships. . . . And the comedy didn't come from one character but from between the characters. That's very unusual for a young writer" (Haller 42). The nature of Henley's dramatic conclusion in *Crimes of the Heart* goes hand-in-hand with her primary focus upon characterization, and her significant break with the tradition of the "well-made play." While the plot moves to a noticeable resolution, with the sisters experiencing a moment of unity they have not thus far experienced in the play, Henley leaves all of the major conflicts primarily unresolved. Stanley Kauffmann wrote in the *Saturday Review* assessment of the Broadway production that "Crimes moves to no real resolution, but this is part of its power. It presents a condition that, in minuscule, implies much about the state of the world, as well as the state of Mississippi, and about human chaos; it says, "Resolution is not my business. Ludicrously horrifying honesty is."

Because of the distinctive balance that Henley strikes—between comedy and tragedy, character and plot, conflict and resolution—the playwright whose technique Henley's most resembles may be Chekhov (although her sense of humor is decidedly more macabre and expressed in more explicit ways). Henley has said of Chekhov's influence upon her that she appreciates how "he doesn't judge people as much as just shows them in the comic and tragic parts of people. Everything's done with such ease, but it hits so deep," as she stated in *Mississippi Writers Talking*. About a production of Chekhov's

*The Cherry Orchard* which particularly moved her, Henley commented in *The Playwright's Art: Conversations with Contemporary American Dramatists* that "It was just absolutely a revelation about how alive life can be and how complicated and beautiful and horrible; to deny either of those is such a loss."

# Historical Context

*Crimes of the Heart,* according to Henley's stage directions, takes place "[i]n the fall, five years after Hurricane Camille." This would set the play in 1974, in the midst of significant upheavals in American society. Henley's characters, however, seem largely unmoved by the events of the outside world, caught up as they are in the pain and disappointment of their personal lives.

## *Vietnam*

The war continued in 1974, setting off a civil war in Cambodia as well. U.S. combat troops had been removed from Vietnam in 1973, although American support of anti-Communist forces in the South of the country continued. Perhaps more important to the American social fabric, the many rifts caused by our involvement in the war in Vietnam were slow to heal. Students and others who had protested against the war remained largely disillusioned about the foreign interests of the U.S. government, and society as a whole remained traumatized by U.S. casualties and the devastation wrought by the war, which had been widely broadcast by the media; the Vietnam War was often referred to as the "living room war" due to the unprecedented level of television coverage.

# Watergate

Perhaps the most significant event in American society in 1974 was the unprecedented resignation of President Richard Nixon, over accusations of his granting approval for the June 17, 1972, burglary of Democratic National Committee offices at the Watergate complex in Washington, D.C. By the end of 1973, a Harris poll suggested that people believed, by a margin of 73 to 21 percent, that the president's credibility had been damaged beyond repair. Like public opinion over Vietnam, Watergate was an important symbol both of stark divisions in American society and a growing disillusionment with the integrity of our leaders. Less than two years after being re-elected in a forty-nine-state landslide and after declaring repeatedly that he would never resign under pressure, Nixon was faced with certain impeachment by Congress. Giving in to the inevitable, he resigned his office in disgrace on August 9.

# World Crises: Food, Energy, Inflation

1974 was an especially trying year for the developing world, as massive famine swept through Asia, South America, and especially Africa, on the heels of drought and several major natural disasters. As they watched this tragedy unfold, citizens of industrialized nations of the West were experiencing social instability of another kind. In the fall of 1973, Arab members of the Organization of Petroleum Exporting Countries (OPEC) leveled an embargo on exports to the Netherlands and the U.S. The United States, with its unparalleled dependency on fuel (in 1974, the nation had six percent of the world's population but consumed thirty-three percent of the world's energy), experienced a severe economic crisis. U.S. economic output for the first quarter of 1974 dropped $10-20 billion, and 500,000 American workers lost their jobs. The U.S. government blamed the Arabs for the crisis, but American public opinion also held U.S. companies responsible for manipulating prices and supplies to corporate advantage. Related to the energy crisis and other factors, the West experienced an inflation crisis as well; annual double-digit inflation became a reality for the first time for most industrial nations.

## *Civil Rights*

On the twenty-year anniversary of the historic Supreme Court decision on school integration, fierce battles were still being fought on the issue, garnering national attention. The conflict centered mostly on issues of school busing, as the site of conflict largely shifted from the South to the cities of the North. In Boston, for example, police had to accompany buses transporting black children to white schools. Meanwhile, baseball player Hank Aaron's breaking of Babe Ruth's career home-run title in 1974 was a significant and uplifting achievement, but its painful post-script—the numerous death threats Aaron received from racists who did not feel it was proper for a black athlete to earn such a title—suggests that bigoted ideas of race in America were, sadly, slow to change.

Growing out of its roots in the 1960s, the movement to define and defend the civil rights of women also continued. 1974 marked a midpoint in the campaign to ratify the Equal Rights Amendment (ERA), which declared: "Equality of rights under the law shall not be denied or abridged by the United States or by any State on account of sex." The amendment was originally passed by the Senate in March, 1972, and by the end of 1974, thirty-one states had ratified it, with a total of thirty-eight needed. Support for the ERA (which eventually failed) was regionally divided: while every state in the Northeast had ratified the amendment by this time, for example, it had been already defeated in Georgia, Florida, and Louisiana. Legislative action was stalled, meanwhile, in many other southern states, including North and South Carolina, Alabama, Mississippi, and Arkansas.

In *Crimes of the Heart,* the characters seem untouched by these prominent events on the national scene. The absence of any prominent historical context to the play may reflect Henley's perspective on national politics: she has described herself as a political cynic with a "moratorium on watching the news since Reagan's been president," as she described herself in *Interviews with Contemporary Women Playwrights*. It may also be a reflection of Henley's perspective on small-town life in the South, where, she feels, people more commonly come together to talk about their own lives and tell stories rather than watch television or discuss the national events being covered in the media. The South of *Crimes of the Heart,* meanwhile, seems largely unaffected by the civil rights movement, large-scale economic development, or other factors of what has often been called an era of unprecedented change in the South.

Regarding the issue of race, for example, consider Babe's affair with Willie Jay, a fifteen-year-old African American youth: while the revelation of it would compromise any case Babe might have against her husband for domestic violence, it presents a greater threat to Willie Jay himself. Because the threat of possible retribution by Zachary or other citizens of the town, Willie Jay has no option but to leave "incognito on the midnight bus—heading North." Henley has made an important observation about race relations in Mississippi, in response to a question actually about recent trends in "colorblind" casting in the theatre. Henley stated in *The Playwright's Art: Conversations with Contemporary American Dramatists* that "it depends on how specific you're being about the character's background as to whether that's an issue." In a play like *Crimes of the Heart,* "if you're writing about a specific time or place . . . then obviously race is important because there is a segregated bigoted thing going on."

# Critical Overview

Beth Henley did not initially have success finding a theatre willing to produce *Crimes of the Heart,* until the play's acceptance by the Actors' Theatre of Louisville. From that point onward, however, the public and critical reception was overwhelmingly positive. Few playwrights achieve such popular success, especially for their first full-length play: a Pulitzer Prize, a Broadway run of more than five hundred performances, a New York Drama Critics Award for best play, a one million dollar Hollywood contract for the screen rights. John Simon's tone is representative of many of the early reviews: writing in the *New York Times* of the off-Broadway production he stated that *Crimes of the Heart* "restores one's faith in our theatre." Simon was, however, wary of being too hopeful about Henley's future success, expressing the fear "that this clearly autobiographical play may be stocked with the riches of youthful memories that many playwrights cannot duplicate in subsequent works."

Reviews of the play on Broadway were also predominantly enthusiastic. Stanley Kauffmann, writing in the *Saturday Review,* found fault with the production itself but found Henley's play powerfully moving. "The play has to fight its way through the opening half hour or so of this production before it lets the author establish what she is getting at—that, under this molasses meandering, there is madness, stark madness."

While Kauffmann did identify some perceived faults in Henley's technique, he stated that overall, "she has struck a rich, if not inexhaustible, dramatic lode." Similarly, Richard Corliss, writing in *Time* magazine, emphasized that Henley's play, with its comedic view of the tragic and grotesque, is deceptively simple: "By the end of the evening, caricatures have been fleshed into characters, jokes into down-home truths, domestic atrocities into strategies for staying alive."

Not all the Broadway reviews, however, were positive. Walter Kerr of the *New York Times* felt that Henley had simply gone too far in her attempts to wring humor out of the tragic, falling into "a beginner's habit of never letting well enough alone, of taking a perfectly genuine bit of observation and doubling and tripling it until it's compounded itself into parody." Throughout the evening, Kerr recalled, "I also found myself, rather too often and in spite of everything, disbelieving—simply and flatly disbelieving." In making his criticism, however, Kerr observed that "this is scarcely the prevailing opinion" on Henley's play. Michael Feingold of the *Village Voice,* meanwhile, was far more vitriolic, stating that the play "gives the impression of gossiping about its characters rather than presenting them. . . never at any point coming close to the truth of their lives." Feingold's opinion, that the "tinny effect of *Crimes of the Heart* is happily mitigated, in the current production, by Melvin Bernhardt's staging" and by the "magical performances" of the cast, is thus diametrically opposed to Kauffmann, who praised the play but criticized the production.

Given Henley's virtually unprecedented success as a young, first-time playwright, and the gap of twenty-three years since another woman had won the Pulitzer Prize for Drama, one of the concerns of critics was to place Henley in the context of other women writing for the stage in the early 1980s. Mel Gussow did so famously in his article "Women Playwrights: New Voices in the Theatre" in the *New York Times Sunday Magazine,* in which he discussed Henley, Marsha Norman, Wendy Wasserstein, Wendy Kesselman, Jane Martin, Emily Mann, and other influential female playwrights. While Gussow's article marked an important transition in the contemporary American theatre, it has been widely rebutted, found by many to be "more notable for its omissions than its conclusions" according to Billy J. Harbin in the *Southern Quarterly.* In particular, critics have been interested in comparing Henley to Norman, another southern woman who won the Pulitzer for Drama (for her play *'night, Mother).* Gussow wrote that among the numerous women finding success as playwrights "the most dissimilar may be Marsha Norman and Beth Henley." Lisa J. McDonnell picked up this theme several years later in an issue of the *Southern Quarterly,* agreeing that there are important differences between the two playwrights, but exploring them in much more depth than Gussow was able to do in his article. At the same time, however, McDonnell observed many important similarities, including "their remarkable gift for storytelling, their use of family drama as a framework, their sensitive delineation of character and relationships, their employment of bizarre Gothic humor and their use of the southern vernacular to demonstrate the poetic lyricism of the commonplace."

The failure of Henley's play *The Wake of Jamey Foster* on Broadway, and the mixed success of her later plays, would seem to lend some credence to John Simon's fear that Henley might never again be able to match the success of *Crimes of the Heart*. While many journalistic critics have been especially hard on Henley's later work, she remains an important figure in the contemporary American theatre. The many published interviews of Henley suggests that she attempts not to take negative reviews to heart: in *The Playwright's Art: Conversations with Contemporary American Dramatists,* she observed with humor that "H. L. Mencken said that asking a playwright what he thinks of critics is like asking a lamppost what he thinks of a dog." *Crimes of the Heart,* meanwhile, has passed into the canon of great American plays, proven by the work of literary critics to be rich and complex enough to support a variety of analytical interpretations. Writing in the *Southern Quarterly,* Nancy Hargrove, for example, examined Henley's vision of human experience in several of her plays, finding it "essentially a tragicomic one, revealing . . . the duality of the universe which inflicts pain and suffering on man but occasionally allows a moment of joy or grace."

Billy Harbin, writing in the *Southern*

*Quarterly,* placed Henley's work in the context of different waves of feminism since the 1960s, exploring the importance of family relationships in her plays. While the family is often portrayed by Henley as simply another source of pain, Harbin felt that *Crimes of the Heart* differs from her other plays in that a "faith in the human spirit. . . can be glimpsed through the sisters' remarkable endurance of suffering and their eventual move toward familial trust and unity." Henley's later characters, according to Harbin, "possess little potential for change," limiting Henley's "success in finding fresh explorations of [her] ideas." With this nuanced view, Harbin nevertheless conforms to the prevailing critical view that Henley has yet to match either the dramatic complexity or the theatrical success of *Crimes of the Heart.* Lou Thompson, in the *Southern Quarterly,* similarly found a sense of unity at the end of the *Crimes of the Heart* but traced its development from of the dominant imagery of food in the play. While the characters eat compulsively throughout, foraging in an attempt "to fill the void in the spirit—a hunger of the heart mistaken for hunger of the stomach," the sisters share Lenny's birthday cake at the end of the play "to celebrate their new lives."

# What Do I Read Next?

- *The Miss Firecracker Contest* (New York: Dramatists Play Service, 1985). Henley's most successful play next to *Crimes of the Heart.* Also set in a small Mississippi town (Brookhaven), it follows the trials and tribulations of Carnelle Scott, a twenty-four-year-old woman with a bad reputation in town who seeks to redeem herself by winning the title of Miss Firecracker for the Fourth of July celebration. With a cast full of very odd characters who, like Carnelle, seek some kind of redemption from their lives, the play probes the grotesque even more so than *Crimes of the Heart.* While some critics have suggested that Henley merely reworks the same ideas from play to play, others have found *The Miss Firecracker Contest* a fresh, original expression of Henley's unique view of life in small southern towns. The play was adapted into a film in 1989, starring Holly Hunter.

- Marsha Norman: *'night, Mother*. Henley and Marsha Norman are often compared and/or contrasted to one another because they each won a Pulitzer Prize for Drama in the early 1980s. Reading this play helps highlight the similarities and differences between the two playwrights.

- Flannery O'Connor: *Collected Works* (New York: Library of America, 1988) and *The Complete Stories* (New York: Farrar, Straus and Giroux, 1971). Reading some of the work of this legendary writer of the "Southern Gothic" tradition, you can judge for yourself the validity of the connections numerous critics have drawn between her work and Henley's plays.

- Carol S. Manning, editor, *The Female Tradition in Southern Literature* (Urbana, IL: University of Illinois Press, 1993). A collection of essays both on specific writers, and on topics such as "Southern Ladies and the Southern Literary Renaissance" and "Spiritual Daughters of the Black American South." Containing extensive analysis of Eudora Welty and Flannery O'Connor, two writers of "Southern Gothic" fiction to whom Henley is often compared, the volume is also is quite useful in placing Henley within a historical continuum of southern women writers, and examining common threads of experience with other writers from whom she differs in other ways.

- John B. Boles, editor, *Dixie Dateline: a Journalistic Portrait of the Contemporary South* (Houston: Rice University Press, 1983). A collection of eleven essays by eminent journalists, presenting a variety of perspectives on the South, its culture, its history, and its future.

# Further Reading

Beaufort, John. "A Play that Proves There's No Explaining Awards" in the *Christian Science Monitor,* November 9, 1981, p. 20.

> A very brief review with a strongly negative opinion of *Crimes of the Heart* that is rare in assessments of Henley's play. Completely dismissing its value, Beaufort wrote that *Crimes of the Heart* is "a perversely antic stage piece that is part eccentric characterization, part Southern fried Gothic comedy, part soap opera, and part patchwork plotting."

Berkvist, Robert. "Act I: The Pulitzer, Act II: Broadway" in the *New York Times,* October 25, 1981, p. D4.

> An article published a week before *Crimes of the Heart's* Broadway opening, containing much of the same biographical information found in more detail in later sources. Berkvist focused on the novelty of a playwright having such success with her first full-length play, and summarizes the positive reception of the play in Louisville and in its Off-Broadway run at the Manhattan

Theatre Club. The article does contain some of Henley's strongest comments on the state of the American theatre, particularly Broadway.

Betsko, Kathleen, and Rachel Koenig. "Beth Henley" in *Interviews with Contemporary Women Playwrights,* Beach Tree Book, 1987, pp. 211-22.

An interview conducted as Henley was completing her play *The Debutante Ball.* Henley discussed her writing and revision process, how she responds to rehearsals and opening nights, her relationship with her own family (fragments of which turn up in all of her plays), and the different levels of opportunity for women and men in the contemporary theatre.

Corliss, Richard. "I Go with What I'm Feeling" in *Time,* February 8, 1982, p. 80.

A brief article published during the successful Broadway run of *Crimes of the Heart* to introduce Henley to a national audience. Corliss stated concisely and cleverly the complexities of Henley's work. "Sugar and spice and every known vice," the article begins; "that's what Beth Henley's plays are made of." Corliss observed that Henley's plays are "deceptively simple. . . . By the end of the evening, caricatures have been fleshed into characters, jokes into down-home truths, domestic atrocities into strategies for staying alive." Henley is quoted in the article stating that "I'm like a child when I write, taking chances, never thinking in terms of logic or reviews. I just go with what I'm feeling." The article documents a moment of new-found success for the young playwright, facing choices about the direction her career will take her.

Feingold, Michael."Dry Roll" in the *Village Voice,* November 18-24, 1981, p. 104.

Perhaps the most negative and vitriolic assessment of *Crimes of the Heart* in print. (The title refers to the musical *Merrily We Roll Along,* which Feingold also discussed in the review.) Feingold finds the play completely disingenuous, even insulting. He wrote that it "gives the impression of gossiping about its characters rather than presenting them . . . never at any point coming close to the truth of their lives." Feingold gave some credit to Henley's "voice" as a playwright, "both individual and skillful," but overall found the play "hollow," something to be overcome by the "magical performances" of the cast.

Gussow, Mel. "Women Playwrights: New Voices in the Theatre" in the *New York Times Sunday Magazine,* May 1, 1983, p. 22.

> Discusses Henley along with numerous other contemporary women playwrights, in an article written on the occasion of Marsha Norman winning the 1983 Pulitzer Prize for Drama. Gussow traced a history of successful women playwrights, including Lillian Hellman in a modern American context, but noted that "not until recently has there been anything approaching a movement." Among the many underlying forces which paved the way for this movement, Gussow mentioned the Actors' Theater of Louisville, where Henley's *Crimes of the Heart* premiered.

Haller, Scott."Her First Play, Her First Pulitzer Prize" in the *Saturday Review,* November, 1981, p. 40.

> Introducing Henley to the public, this brief article was published just prior to *Crimes of the Heart* opening on Broadway. Haller marveled at the success achieved by a young "29-

year-old who had never before written a full-length play." Based on an interview with the playwright, the article is primarily biographical, suggesting how being raised in the South provides Henley both with material and a vernacular speech. This theatrical dialect, combined with Henley's "unlikely dramatic alliance" between "the conventions of the naturalistic play" and "the unconventional protagonists of absurdist comedy" gives Henley what Haller called her "idiosyncratic voice," which audiences have found so refreshing.

Harbin, Billy J. "Familial Bonds in the Plays of Beth Henley" in the *Southern Quarterly,* Vol. 25, no. 3, 1987, pp. 80-94.

Harbin begins by placing Henley's work in the context of different waves of feminism since the 1960s.

Hargrove, Nancy D. "The Tragicomic Vision of Beth Henley's Drama" in the *Southern Quarterly,* Vol. 22, no. 4, 1984, pp. 80-94.

Hargrove examines Henley's first three full-length plays, exploring (as the title suggests) the powerful mixture of tragedy and comedy within each.

Heilpern, John. "Great Acting, Pity about the Play"

in the London *Times,* December 5, 1981, p. 11.

> A review of three Broadway productions, with brief comments on *Crimes of the Heart.* "I regret," Heilpern wrote, "it left me mostly cold." It is interesting to consider whether, as Heilpern mused, he found the play bizarre and unsatisfying because as a British critic he suffered from "a serious culture gap." Instead of a complex, illuminating play (as so many American critics found *(Crimes of the Heart),* Heilpern saw only "unbelievable 'characters' whose lives were a mere farce. I could see only Southern 'types', like a cartoon."

Jones, John Griffin. "Beth Henley" in *Mississippi Writers Talking,* University Press of Mississippi, 1982, pp. 169-90.

> A rare interview conducted *before* Henley won the Pulitzer Prize for *Crimes of the Heart.* As such, it focuses on many biographical details from Henley's life, which had not yet received a great deal of public attention.

Kauffmann, Stanley. "Two Cheers for Two Plays" in the *Saturday Review,* Vol. 9, no. 1, 1982, pp. 54-55.

A review of the Broadway production of *Crimes of the Heart*. Kauffmann praised the play but says its success "is, to some extent, a victory over this production." Kauffmann identified some faults in the play (such as the amount of action which occurs offstage and is reported) but overall his review is full of praise.

Kerr, Walter. "Offbeat—but a Beat Too Far" in the *New York Times,* November 15, 1981, p. D3.

In this review of the Broadway production of *Crimes of the Heart,* Kerr's perspective on the play is a mixed one. He offers many examples to support his opinion. Kerr is insightful about the delicate balance Henley strikes in her play—between humor and tragedy, between the hurtful actions of some the characters and the positive impressions of them the audience is nevertheless expected to maintain.

McDonnell, Lisa J. "Diverse Similitude: Beth Henley and Marsha Norman" in the *Southern Quarterly,* Vol. 25, no. 3, 1987, pp. 95-104.

A comparison and contrasting of the techniques of southern playwrights Henley and Norman, who won the Pulitzer Prize for Drama within two years of one another. The playwrights share "their remarkable gift for storytelling, their use of family drama as a framework, their sensitive delineation of character and relationships, their employment of bizarre Gothic humor and their use of the southern vernacular to demonstrate the poetic lyricism of the commonplace." Despite the similarities between them (which do go far beyond being southern women playwrights who have won the Pulitzer), McDonnell concluded that "they have already, relatively early in their playwriting careers, set themselves on paths that are likely to become increasingly divergent."

Oliva, Judy Lee. "Beth Henley" in *Contemporary Dramatists,* 5th edition, St. James Press, 1993. 290-91.

A more recent assessment which includes Henley's play *Abundance,* an epic play spanning 25 years in the lives of two pioneer women in the nineteenth century. Oliva examined what she calls a "unifying factor" in Henley's plays: "women who seek to define themselves outside of their relationships with men and beyond their family environment." In Oliva's assessment, "it is Henley's characters

> who provide unique contributions to the dramaturgy." As important to Henley's plays as the characters are the stories they tell,"especially those stories in which female characters can turn to other female characters for help."

Simon, John. "Sisterhood is Beautiful" in the *New York Times,* January 12, 1981, pp. 42-44.

> A glowing review of the off-Broadway production of *Crimes of the Heart,* which "restores one's faith in our theatre."

Thompson, Lou. "Feeding the Hungry Heart: Food in Beth Henley's *Crimes of the Heart"* in the *Southern Quarterly,* Vol. 30, nos. 2-3, 1992, pp. 99-102.

> Drawing from Nancy Hargrove's observation in an earlier article that eating and drinking are, in Henley's plays, "among the few pleasures in life, or, in certain cases, among the few consolations *for* life," Thompson explored in more detail the pervasive imagery of food throughout *Crimes of the Heart.*

Willer-Moul, Cynthia. "Beth Henley" in *The Playwright's Art: Conversations with Contemporary American Dramatists,* Rutgers University Press, 1995, pp. 102-22.

A much more recent source, this interview covers a wider range of Henley's works, but still contains detailed discussion of *Crimes of the Heart*. Henley talks extensively about her writing process, from fundamental ideas to notes and outlines, the beginnings of dialogue, revisions, and finally rehearsals and the production itself.